Bear Cub

AT HOME IN THE FOREST

WRITTEN BY SARAH TOAST
ILLUSTRATED BY KRISTA BRAUCKMANN-TOWNS

1.

As summer draws to an end, Mother Bear roams through the mountain forest, gathering and eating enormous amounts of berries and fruit.

Mother Bear is putting on fat so she can sleep in her den the entire winter. The layer of fat is to keep her warm and help her provide rich milk for the baby bear that will be born.

Mother Bear chooses a rocky cave to be her den during the winter. Inside the den, she and her baby will be protected from the cold wind and blowing snow. She pads it with moss, leaves, and grass to make it warm and soft for herself and the baby.

As the first flakes of winter snow begin to fall, Mother Bear settles down to sleep.

In the middle of winter, when the snow drifts are deep outside the den, Mother Bear's tiny cub is born. With closed eyes and hardly any fur, the cub will grow quickly, nourished by Mother Bear's rich milk.

Baby Bear and Mother Bear sleep on, but Mother Bear will wake up and protect him if the winter home is disturbed.

In a few weeks, Baby Bear's eyes open. He is now covered in thick, soft fur. Mother Bear and Baby Bear stay in their snug den another month.

In the spring, Baby Bear and his mother emerge from the den. Mother Bear shows Baby Bear how to look through the forest for tender shoots that will make a good meal.

Mother Bear makes her way with Baby Bear down the grassy slope to the elks' winter range. She lifts up her head and sniffs the breeze. Baby Bear moves his raised head back and forth so hard he falls over.

Mother Bear finds an elk that died in the winter when the snows were deep and not enough food could be found.

Mother Bear eats what she can of the nourishing elk meat. Then she buries it in a shallow hole and covers it with leaves, twigs, and dirt. She will return to it later.

Baby Bear learns by watching what his mother does. The most important rules for Baby Bear to learn are to follow mother, obey mother, and have fun.

Mother Bear teaches her cub to turn over fallen branches and look for grubs to eat. With their long, sharp claws, Baby Bear and Mother Bear dig up bulbs, roots, and snails.

When his mother stops to rest, Baby Bear climbs all over her. He somersaults into her lap and nibbles her ears, then runs off to chase a field mouse.

When Mother Bear looks up from playing with her cub, she sees that a lean wolf is watching her and Baby Bear. Quickly she chases the cub into a hollow tree stump. Then she turns to face the wolf.

Mother Bear stands up on her hind legs, swings her front paws, and roars a loud growl. The wolf runs away.

Mother Bear calls to her cub, but he doesn't come out of the hollow stump. Mother Bear goes to find out why.

Baby Bear has found a treat. It is a honeycomb with honey from last summer still inside. Baby Bear sticks his little paw in the honeycomb and licks it. He tastes the wildflowers of summer in the sweet honey.

When Baby Bear backs out of the hollow log, he brings some tasty honeycomb for his mother. She happily eats the honey, and then she and her cub give each other a true bear hug.